BBC earth

DO YOU KNOW?

Level 3

MAMMALS

Inspired by BBC Earth TV series and developed with input from BBC Earth natural history specialists

Written by Sarah Wassner-Flynn
Text adapted by Catrin Morris
Series Editor: Nick Coates

LADYBIRD BOOKS

UK | USA | Canada | Ireland | Australia
India | New Zealand | South Africa

Ladybird Books is part of the Penguin Random House group of companies
whose addresses can be found at global.penguinrandomhouse.com.
www.penguin.co.uk   www.puffin.co.uk   www.ladybird.co.uk

Penguin
Random House
UK

First published 2020
001

Printed in China

A CIP catalogue record for this book is available from the British Library

ISBN: 978–0–241–38285–1

All correspondence to:
Ladybird Books Ltd
Penguin Random House Children's
One Embassy Gardens, New Union Square
5 Nine Elms Lane, London SW8 5DA

Contents

New words

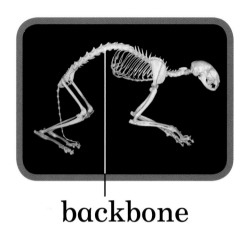

backbone

be born

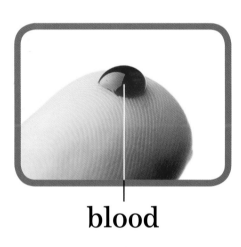

blood

breathe

chew

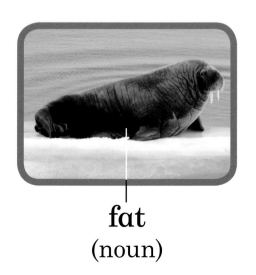

fat
(noun)

forest

hoof
(hooves)

insect

land
(noun)

marine

tongue

What is a mammal?

A mammal has hair and a **backbone**.

Some animals come out of eggs,
but most mammals do not.

Mammals are warm when it is cold outside.
This is because they
have warm **blood**.

Polar bears are mammals.
They stay warm in the cold.

Mammals drink their mother's milk when they **are born**.

Elephants are mammals. The mothers can have one baby every five years.

THINK!

Write the names of ten mammals.
What is the same about these animals?
What is different about them?

Where do mammals live?

Mammals live all across the world.

Most mammals live on **land**, but some live in water.

Mammals live in hot and cold places.

An orca is a mammal that lives in the sea. Orcas are part of the dolphin family.

A zebra likes living where there is grass or sand.

Mammals live in **forests**, in mountains, in deserts and even in cities.

LOOK!

Look at the pages.
Where do you find mammals in the world?

Do all mammals eat meat?

Different animals
eat different food.

Bears and people
eat plants and meat.
They are called omnivores.

Giraffes and horses only
eat plants. They are
called herbivores.

Lions and tigers only eat meat. They are called carnivores.

Lions use their teeth to kill other animals for food.

Hedgehogs eat **insects**. They are called insectivores.

WATCH!

Watch the video (see page 32).
What are the bears trying to catch and eat?

How do mammals stay warm?

Most mammals have fur or hair on their bodies. People do, too!

It helps them to stay warm in cold places.

fur

An Arctic wolf has two fur coats. They help the wolf to stay warm when it is very cold.

Dolphins and whales are **marine** mammals. They are born with hair on their noses, but they lose it when they are older.

They also have **fat**, called blubber. This stops them getting too cold in the water.

LOOK!

Look at the pages.
What colour is the Arctic wolf?
How can this colour help the wolf?

How many different mammals are there?

There are more than 5000 different kinds of mammals on Earth.

There are different families of mammals.

People, monkeys, apes and lemurs are called primates.

Mice and rats are called rodents.

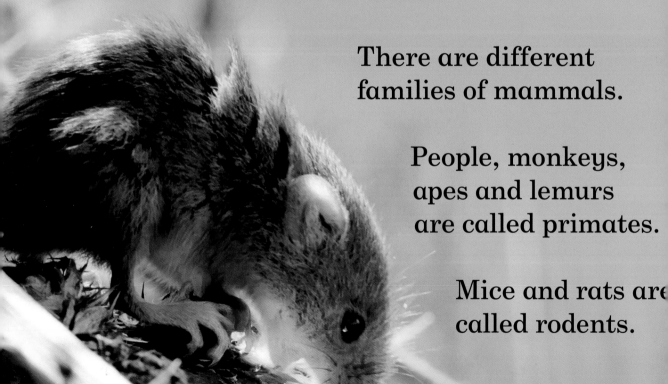

Deer and giraffes are called ungulates. They have hard feet called **hooves**.

Antelopes are also ungulates.

Whales and dolphins, which are marine mammals, are called cetaceans.

 PROJECT

Work in a group.
Use books or the internet to find five mammals from each family (primates, rodents, ungulates and cetaceans). How are the animals in every family the same? How are the families different?

Do baby mammals come from eggs?

Only platypus and echidna babies come from eggs.

This is a platypus.

Other baby mammals do not come from eggs. The mother carries her baby inside her body.

When the baby is born, the mother gives her milk to it.

Young bonobos stay near their mothers. The mothers can carry their babies and give them milk for up to five years.

This is an echidna.

FIND OUT!

Use books or the internet to find out what baby echidnas are called. Do they look like their mothers?

Can mammals breathe underwater?

All mammals **breathe**.
Marine mammals have to breathe, too.

Fish can breathe under the water,
but mammals cannot.

Humpback whales come up to breathe. They breathe in and out of a hole in the top of their heads.

Dolphins, whales and seals can stay underwater for one hour or more, but they always come up to breathe.

Elephant seals can stay underwater for two hours.

LOOK!

Look at the pages.
Can marine mammals breathe underwater?
How many hours can they stay underwater for?

Can mammals fly?

Bats are the only mammals that can fly.

They use their wings to fly.

Bats have long, thin wings that can help them to fly very fast.

Other mammals don't have wings and they can't really fly.

But they can jump a very long way.

Flying squirrels move from tree to tree. A part of their coat is like a wing.

 LOOK!

Look at the pages.
Can flying squirrels fly?
How do they move from tree to tree?

Which mammals do not chew their food?

Most mammals **chew** their food with their teeth.

Tigers can kill other animals and eat the meat with their strong teeth and mouths.

A few mammals do not have any teeth.

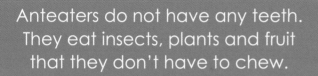

Anteaters do not have any teeth. They eat insects, plants and fruit that they don't have to chew.

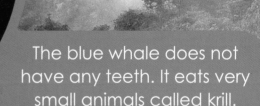

The blue whale does not have any teeth. It eats very small animals called krill.

▶ WATCH!

Watch the video (see page 32).
How does the whale eat the krill?

23

How clever is a chimpanzee?

Mammals are very clever. Chimpanzees are some of the cleverest mammals.

Chimpanzees can understand some words. They also play with sticks.

Chimpanzees can use things that they find in the forest to catch and eat insects, too.

Chimpanzees use their faces and make noises to talk to other chimpanzees.

WATCH!

Watch the video (see page 32).
How does the chimpanzee catch its food?
Why is the chimpanzee clever?

What are the biggest and smallest mammals?

Mammals can be big or small, long or short.

A blue whale's **tongue** is as heavy as an elephant!

The smallest mammal on Earth is the Etruscan shrew. It is smaller than your little finger.

The blue whale is the biggest mammal on Earth.

It can be as heavy as three big lorries and as long as two buses.

FIND OUT!

Use books or the internet to find out which other mammals are very big or very small.

What are the fastest and slowest mammals?

The cheetah is the fastest mammal on Earth.

When it is running after other animals, it can move faster than a car.

Cheetahs can catch food because they run very quickly.

Sloths move more slowly than any other animal on Earth.

In one day, they only move about 50 metres. Most people can move 50 metres in one minute!

Sloths move very slowly, but they can swim well.

PROJECT

Work in a group.
Use books or the internet to find out about the fastest five mammals on Earth.
Talk about them with your friends.
Why are they fast?

29

Quiz

Choose the correct answers.

1 Which sentence is NOT true?
  a All mammals have a backbone.
  b All mammals drink their mother's milk.
  c All mammals have no hair.

2 Which sentence is NOT true?
  a All mammals live on land.
  b Most mammals live on land.
  c Some mammals live in water.

3 Which sentence is NOT true?
  a Carnivores only eat meat.
  b Omnivores eat meat and plants.
  c Insectivores only eat plants.

4 How many different kinds of mammals are there?
  a less than 500
  b more than 5000
  c more than 50000

5 Which sentence is true?

  a All mammals come from eggs.

  b Most mammals come from eggs.

  c A few mammals come from eggs.

6 Which sentence is true?

  a Fish and mammals can breathe under the water.

  b Fish and mammals cannot breathe under the water.

  c Fish can breathe under the water, but mammals cannot.

7 Which mammal can fly?

  a a bat

  b a flying squirrel

  c a platypus

8 Which sentence is true?

  a All mammals have teeth.

  b Most mammals have teeth.

  c No mammals have teeth.

Visit www.ladybirdeducation.co.uk for FREE DO YOU KNOW? teaching resources.

- video clips with simplified voiceover and subtitles
- video and comprehension activities
- class projects and lesson plans
- audio recording of every book
- digital version of every book
- full answer keys

To access video clips, audio tracks and digital books:

1 Go to **www.ladybirdeducation.co.uk**
2 Click "Unlock book"
3 Enter the code below

FCFsVpMbBv

Stay safe online! Some of the DO YOU KNOW? activities ask children to do extra research online. Remember:

- ensure an adult is supervising;
- use established search engines such as Google or Kiddle;
- children should never share personal details, such as name, home or school address, telephone number or photos.